BASKETBALL'S
BEST SHOTS

THE GREATEST NBA® PHOTOGRAPHY OF THE CENTURY

BASKETBALL'S
BEST SHOTS

THE GREATEST NBA® PHOTOGRAPHY
OF THE CENTURY

FOREWORD BY WALT "CLYDE" FRAZIER

DK PUBLISHING

BASKETBALL'S BEST SHOTS

A DK PUBLISHING BOOK

DK Publishing, Inc.
375 Hudson Street
New York, NY 10014

00 01 02 03 04 05 10 9 8 7 6 5 4 3 2 1

DK Publishing, Inc.:
Publisher: Chuck Lang
Editorial Director: Chuck Wills
Creative Director: Tina Vaughan
Art Director: Dirk Kaufman
Designer: Jon Glick
Production Manager: Chris Avgherinos
DTP Coordinator: Milos Orlovic

Color reproduction by ColourScan, Singapore
Printed and bound by Toppan, China

NATIONAL BASKETBALL ASSOCIATION

The NBA and individual NBA member team identifications reproduced in and on this publication are the property of NBA Properties, Inc. and the respective NBA member teams and may not be used, in whole or in part, without the written consent of NBA Properties, Inc.

NBA Publishing: Charles Rosenzweig, Mario Argote, John Hareas, Michael Levine, David Mintz
NBA Entertainment Photos: Carmin Romanelli, Joe Amati, David Bonilla, Pam Costello, Mike Klein, John Kristofick, Bennett Renda, Brian Choi, Scott Yurdin
NBA Entertainment: Adam Silver, Gregg Winik, Paul Hirschheimer, Zelda Spoelstra, Marc Hirschheimer, Meredith Tanchum
Photo Editor: Joe Amati
Writer: John Hareas

NBA Entertainment Staff Photographers: Andrew D. Bernstein, Nathaniel S. Butler, Jesse D. Garrabrant

GATEFOLD PAGES 91-92 (NBA AT 50)
First Row (left to right): Paul Arizin, Bill Sharman, Nate Archibald, Isiah Thomas, Sam Jones, John Stockton, Clyde Frazier, Bob Cousy, Dave Bing, Oscar Robertson, Bob Pettit and Dolph Schayes. Second Row (left to right): Kareem Abdul-Jabbar, Lenny Wilkens, Earl Monroe, John Havlicek, Magic Johnson, Michael Jordan, Larry Bird, Hal Greer, Clyde Drexler and Rick Barry. Third row (left to right): George Mikan, Wes Unseld, Julius Erving, Elgin Baylor, George Gervin, Dave DeBusschere, James Worthy, Charles Barkley and Nate Thurmond. Fourth Row (left to right): Scottie Pippen, Patrick Ewing, Jerry Lucas, Hakeem Olajuwon, Robert Parish, Dave Cowens, Billy Cunningham, Elvin Hayes, Karl Malone, Kevin McHale, David Robinson, Bill Russell, Moses Malone, Willis Reed, Wilt Chamberlain and Bill Walton.

PHOTO CREDITS
Ray Amati: 132; Victor Baldizon: 155; Bill Baptist: 43,99,110; Randy Belice: 34-35,119; Andrew D. Bernstein: 12-13,18,19,27,28-29,42,48-49, 54-55,58,59,66,69,78,93,100,104,112,116,118,122,123,138,142,150,153,156,158-159; Nathaniel S. Butler: 30, 38, 40, 41, 56, 60, 61, 65, 70, 72, 73, 74-75, 91-92, 97, 105, 117, 121, 125, 130, 145, 152, 160, Jim Cummins: 87-90,131; Gary Dineen: 17,144; Garrett W. Ellwood: 76,149; 152: D. Clarke Evans: 26; Sam Forencich: 20-21,33,37,38,44-45,67,101,114-115,148;Greg Foster: 31,79; Jesse D. Garrabrant: Cover,16,94-95; 126,137,139; Barry Gossage: 108, 120, 157; Andy Hayt: 5,38,57,82,113,135; Michael Hoiland: 1; Walter Iooss, Jr.: Title,7,22,23,62-63,98,146-147; Glenn James: 140,154; George Kalinsky: 24-25,52,64; Neil Leifer: 39,77,106-107,128-129; Tim Mantoani: 134; Fernando Medina: 81, 85-86,133,136; Peter Read Miller: 15; Robert Mora: 32,47; NBA Photo Library: 143; Anthony Neste:141; Norm Perdue: 80,111,127; Jennifer Pottheiser: 84, 152; Dick Raphael: 71; Ken Regan: 53, Jacket; Wen Roberts: 14; David Sherman: 46; Noren Trotman: 124; Jeff Vinnick: 109; Jerry Wachter: 68; Rocky Widner: 36, 50,51,83,96, 102,103; Steve Woltmann: 151

POSITIVE VIBE
PAGE 1:
JASON KIDD'S POSITIVE ENERGY AND ELECTRIFIED AURA ARE CAPTURED BY PHOTOGRAPHER AND ARTIST MICHAEL HOILAND. UTILIZING A DIVERSE PALLET OF VIBRANT COLORS, LINEAR DESIGNS AND LIGHT PAINTING, HOILAND EXECUTES HIS POSITIVE ENERGY MESSAGE, WHICH IS CAPTURED COMPLETELY IN CAMERA, WITHOUT ANY COMPUTER ASSISTANCE.

YOUTHFUL EXUBERANCE
PAGES 2-3:
THE CHARISMA, CONFIDENCE, AND ATHLETICISM OF KEVIN GARNETT PRACTICALLY JUMPS OFF THE PAGE IN THIS WALTER IOOSS, JR. PORTRAIT.

TORCH BEARERS
OPPOSITE:
BASKETBALL GENERATIONS CROSS PATHS IN THIS PORTRAIT TAKEN PRIOR TO THE 2002 NBA ALL-STAR GAME IN PHILADELPHIA. TWO OF TODAY'S BRIGHTEST SUPERSTARS, KOBE BRYANT AND KEVIN GARNETT, FLANK LEGENDARY SUPERSTAR, MICHAEL JORDAN.

POETRY BRILLIANTLY CAPTURED

BY WALT "CLYDE" FRAZIER

ONE OF THE MOST frequently asked questions people pose to me is: "Hey, Clyde. Where's the mink coat?" Or, "Where's the Rolls?" It's inevitable. It doesn't matter where I am. I could be walking on the streets of New York City or relaxing somewhere in Florida and people still identify me with the sartorial splendor of my alter ego, Clyde. It's astonishing, even kids who weren't born when I played for the New York Knicks will come up to me and say, "Hey, man. Clyde, you were *so* cool." Even though it's been 30-plus years since the genesis of the Clyde style, I have the power of photography to thank for keeping the legacy alive.

One of the photos people best remember and one of my all-time favorites is the one featured on this book's inside back jacket. It truly captures the essence of the Clyde stratosphere and all of his fashion brilliance and creativity. There I am, confidently posing with a basketball in front of my Rolls Royce, which features a vanity license plate—WCF—while wearing a Borsalino hat made of brown velour and an elephant coat. I have New York City behind me, the town that embraced and embellished the Clyde legend. Every time I look at this photo, I think to myself, "N.Y.'s my town, man. I'm Clyde. I control N.Y., basketball, and fashion."

The Clyde image transcended basketball, thanks to photography. All of my endorsements dealt with Clyde, from Puma sneakers to fur coats, and so did the fashion photo shoots I did for a variety of magazines including *Vogue, Playboy, Ebony,* and *Jet.* Clyde operated from 12:00 A.M. to 4:00 A.M. and the rest of the day I was Walt, resting and waiting for Clyde to emerge. Walt was quiet and shy. Clyde sought the limelight and wanted to be seen around town. Even people who didn't follow the game knew about Clyde from the photo layouts they saw in magazines.

These photos added and enhanced the Clyde mystique and are forever etched in people's minds. Sure, fans remember me as a two-time NBA champion with the Knicks, but a lot of today's players remember me as the sex symbol from the '70s as much as an All-Star point guard for the Knicks. It's funny. Corporations spend millions and billions of dollars trying to perfect an image and, unknowingly, I did it with the help of photography.

What's extraordinary about this book, *Basketball's Best Shots,* is that not only is it a celebration of the NBA's best photos, but it also preserves the legacy of the great NBA moments and players for fans of today and tomorrow to enjoy. Some of the most memorable images are taken from my era as a player. I find myself staring at the athletic grace and flexibility of Bill Russell pulling down a rebound with his left leg practically behind his head in one photo, while enviously looking at another photo of him holding all of his championship rings. The expression on his face says it all. "Eat your heart out, fellas. I've got all of the gold here." I bet his famous, infectious cackle was heard after this photo was taken.

When I look at the famous Willis Reed Game 7 photo from the 1970 NBA Finals—astutely taken by the Knicks team photographer George Kalinsky—I still hear the roar of the Garden crowd ringing in my ears. That moment brings back wonderful memories for me. I remember we were all warming up prior to tip-off and all of a sudden you heard this eruption from the crowd as my teammate valiantly made his way onto the court. I'll never forget, the Lakers stopped warming up to take a look as the thrilling drama was unfolding. Three of the 50 Greatest Players in NBA History—Elgin Baylor, Wilt Chamberlain, and Jerry West—were mesmerized in stunned disbelief as they stood and watched Willis.

No other sport unequivocally accentuates athletic beauty and grace while lending itself to dramatic and awe-inspiring photography than the NBA and the players featured in the pages of this book. It's poetry in motion, man. Dr. J was like a 747 going up for a dunk, displaying an enormous wingspan and palming the basketball like a grapefruit as he made yet another stylish house call on an opponent. Or marvel at the reckless abandon displayed by Dennis Rodman as he completely lays himself out in his overzealous pursuit of a loose ball, an astounding play that speaks of his hustle, his work ethic, and the tenacity that made him the player he was. And what about the showmanship of Vince Carter displaying the between-the-legs provocative dunk that set him apart from the Doctor and Michael Jordan in showing his own original

style? All of these players exhibited their individual style of mind-numbing athleticism captured in a millisecond by talented photographers who had the creative sense to capture just the right moment. As a Knicks broadcaster covering 82 regular-season games, I'm treated to electrifying, gravity-defying, mesmerizing athletic brilliance on a nightly basis.

The power of photography is also illustrated in behind-the-scenes moments as well. One of the most indelible images in recent memory is an overwhelmed Michael Jordan hugging his first NBA championship trophy in the locker room as his late father stands by his side to comfort him. Here's the greatest player in the game overcome with emotion, which speaks volumes about how much winning means to him. He just reached the pinnacle, yet he still found solace in his father's comfort. This photo makes the superhuman Jordan appear human, man.

All of these photos are visual icons of not only the players but also their respective eras. Decades from now, there will be a young fan who will immerse himself in learning about this exquisite game, and he will come across the names of Wilt Chamberlain, Julius Erving, Larry Bird, or Magic Johnson. And those players will come to life in this book of stirring, captivating images.

If I could do it all over again, I would relish the moments more from my playing days. I took it all for granted—the championships and the individual awards—because when you're playing, you never see the end coming. For me, *Basketball's Best Shots* preserves the memories of the Knicks' accomplishments while also enhancing the legacy of the NBA's glorious past and present. Who knows: Fifty years from now, someone will look at the photo of Clyde in front of his Rolls and say, *"Man, that cat had style."*

Walt "Clyde" Frazier

INTRODUCTION
MAGIC MOMENTS
BY CARMIN ROMANELLI,
SENIOR DIRECTOR, NBA ENTERTAINMENT PHOTOS

A MAGICAL QUALITY OF PHOTOGRAPHY is its unique ability to capture and forever preserve a moment of time. Part of a photographer's skill lies in his or her ability to be decisive at the precise instant necessary to capture the most compelling moment of an action. The photographers working for NBA Entertainment and those featured in this book excel at doing just that—capturing magical moments.

These photographers are also very fortunate because they photograph amazing athletes performing feats of physical prowess often combined with the grace usually associated with ballet. In fact, like ballet, basketball is indeed a performance art, but it is an art performed during the intense competition of contesting a game. Unlike athletes in other sports, NBA players don't use any protective gear. Free from helmets and pads, their sculpted bodies are on display communicating, the intensity of the competition with unequaled body language—as demonstrated in photographs of players such as Kobe Bryant and Dennis Rodman.

Preparation is key for the photographers. They arrive early, meticulously positioning their cameras to capture that night's performance. Unlike a scripted theatrical performance, each moment of an NBA game is unpredictable, requiring the photographer to always be prepared to capture the next magical moment.

When they are not shooting game action, NBA Entertainment Photographers try to tap into a player's personality in specially arranged portrait shoots. Whether it's the enthusiasm and exuberance of Magic Johnson or the ice-sculptured basketballs palmed by former great George Gervin, if a photographer does his or her job well, personalities come alive in these portraits.

Choosing the photographs for *Basketball's Best Shots* was a daunting task because photography and a viewer's reaction to a photograph are both so subjective. This, combined with the fact that the NBA Entertainment Photo Archive features more than 3 million images, there were a lot of difficult decisions to make. Additionally, each season NBA Entertainment Photographers shoot well over one million new images that are expertly edited to the 75,000 selects, which live on in the archive. All of the people who worked on this book can only hope that we delivered some of your favorite magical moments.

Previewed in this introduction are some of *Best Shots'* most memorable images. These classic, breathtaking photographs truly represent the spirit of this book. The photographers, many of whom have covered the NBA for many years, share their insight into how these moments were captured. We hope you enjoy this photographic journey as much as we enjoyed putting it together for you. Please share the magic.

I WAS IN MIDST of a chaotic championship locker room celebration scene at the Great Western Forum. The room appeared to be the size of a closet and was overflowing with media, family members, and champagne. As the official NBA photographer, I was shooting the Chicago Bulls championship trophy presentation standing on a folding bridge table trying to get any picture that I could. Suddenly, I'm thinking, "Where's Michael?" I looked around and couldn't find him. It turned out he was directly behind me, holding the trophy, crying while his dad is consoling him. I saw this and it appeared almost incongruous because you're used to athletes going crazy, celebrating in the locker room. There isn't much feeling behind it, just pure excitement. This,

however, was an actual moment you can feel. So I took the picture and because I was shooting from above, I was able to frame it so that it looked like he and his dad were alone despite the locker room hysteria. A few seconds after I took the photo, the media converged on Michael and the moment was gone.

This is a very important picture to Michael because of what it represents professionally and personally. He has told me that he considers this picture timeless and historic because of his father's presence. Those words mean a lot to me because I share a close relationship with my father that I value greatly.

—*Andrew D. Bernstein,*
NBA Senior Official Staff Photographer

I HAVE TAKEN PICTURES for 40 years but the night I photographed Kevin Garnett at Ice Box Studios in Minneapolis was one of the best nights I have had picture wise in my career. For me, some real landmark photos were taken that night.

I was shooting a Garnett cover story for *Sports Illustrated* and wanted to experiment with some different approaches. I like to take chances when I'm shooting so I used a high-contrast Kodak film called Technopan. I had never used this film before but it has an incredible quality to it. It can make a good picture great and an ordinary picture interesting. I was shooting in an all-white studio and I laid the strobe on

the ground so I can get the shadow off the white wall. I took some Polaroids of my assistant and thought they looked good but when Kevin arrived, it was mind-boggling.

What struck me about this photo is the elongated shape of Kevin's body, the definition of his arms, his skin, which we oiled, and his animated facial expression. Not every athlete is free to make that face. Kevin's youthful confidence clearly comes across in this photograph. He has such a natural sense of film. If I had someone else leaping there, the image probably would not have been half as good. It's just one of those perfect shots.

—*Walter Iooss, Jr.*

AS MICHAEL JORDAN dribbled toward destiny with the final seconds of Game 6 ticking away, I checked my framing and focus, then waited. Everyone in the packed Delta Center anticipated that Michael would shoot the potential game winner and I needed to be ready for that possible buzzer-beating shot. I made sure the photo would include the shooter, shot clock and court with the Jazz fans creating a human backdrop. My camera was part of a system of electronically linked cameras activated by fellow NBA photographer Andy Bernstein. My preparation, along with his timing,

worked flawlessly together as my camera froze this memorable MJ moment.

Aside from Michael's dramatic heroics, what makes this shot fascinating is the multitude of facial expressions seen on the fans behind the basket. It's an interesting study of humanity. You have fans screaming, thinking they can distract Michael, while others hold their heads or faces, fearing the worst. Some seem resigned to the outcome, while others anxiously watch, allowing the moment to unfold. A neat part of this picture is the little boy to the right of the backboard,

wearing a black Bulls' jersey and confidently signaling that the shot is good. Without this myriad of reactions, this photo wouldn't have been nearly as compelling.

—*Fernando Medina, NBA Photographer*

IVERSON VS. CARTER: A rivalry was born and this image captures the intensity displayed by both players during the 2001 Eastern Conference Semifinals. I took this photograph in Game 1 and it's symbolic of how the series went. Both players and teams went all out but as the image reveals, Allen and the Sixers had the inside track on Vince and the Raptors. Both Allen and Vince put on quit a show that series. Each player scored 50 or more points in consecutive games. This image also speaks to the heart and determination of Allen, who is barely 6-0 yet has no fear in driving to the basket.

This photograph also holds special significance for me because it made the cover of *Sports Illustrated* later that week. Not only was that quite an honor, especially since it was my first *SI* cover, but it was

made even more special in the way in which I received the news. Manny Milan, longtime photographer for *Sports Illustrated*, who was actually at the game shooting along the baseline, surprised me and presented me with a copy of the magazine prior to Game 2. I also received congratulatory calls from NBA colleagues and senior official photographers Nat Butler and Andy Bernstein, two professionals who I have admired and learned from throughout my career. I also heard from world renowned photographer Neil Leifer. It was a moving moment for me to be congratulated by my esteemed photographers.

—*Jesse D. Garrabrant, NBA Photographer*

IN MY 35 YEARS covering events at Madison Square Garden, I have never witnessed a more electrifying moment than the night Willis Reed heroically limped out onto the court in Game 7 of the 1970 NBA

Finals. There was an air of uncertainty prior to that game. The No. 1 question on everyone's minds in New York that day was, "Is Willis going to play?" Willis told me earlier that if he could walk, he was going to play. Sure enough as players from both the Knicks and Lakers were warming up, Willis was getting dressed and told me, "Let's go. We're going to win a championship tonight."

As we walked toward the court, the crowd noticed the Knicks' captain. The cheer from the 19,000-plus fans grew into a thunderous ovation. I have never heard the Garden more passionate and intense than

that night. Originally, I wasn't thinking about taking Willis' photo. I was more concerned about his well being, but the crowd clearly brought another dimension to this moment. I jumped about 10-15 feet in front of Willis and took one photo of him before he stepped onto the court. The only other shot that I took was this one featured. In my mind, it captures the extraordinary courage of Willis inspiring his team to victory. It also captured the state of euphoria experienced in the Garden at that precise moment in time.

—*George Kalinsky, New York Knicks Team Photographer*

MY MUHAMMAD ALI-Sonny Liston photograph, which many consider one of the best sports pictures of all time, is not—believe or not—my personal all-time favorite picture. Why then is the picture so popular? I think it's because it captures the essence and spirit of Ali in a manner that clearly portrays him in a way that most people want to remember the boxing legend. Similar to that photograph, people love my Julius Erving picture. But to me, it is just another basketball picture. Obviously, it strikes a chord with others who have told me, that like the Ali-Liston

picture, it captures the style and grace that personified the basketball legend. It's the way people want to remember Dr. J. It's funny because before I closed my recently published book, *The Best of Leifer*, I had many people tell me, "Why aren't you using the Julius Erving dunk photograph?" It is maybe my best-known basketball picture yet it didn't come close to making the cut for my (Best of) book. I don't even consider it my best pro basketball picture. But other people do and that's certainly good enough for me.

—*Neil Leifer*

A SIGNIFICANT PART of my childhood was spent following the NBA. I have a lot of wonderful memories watching the game's all-time greats play such as Oscar Robertson, Clyde Frazier, Wilt Chamberlain, and others. So, when I received the opportunity to photograph

these legends along with others for the NBA at 50 portrait shoot in Cleveland during the 1997 NBA All-Star Weekend, I knew it would be special.

The magnitude of the photo shoot really hit me earlier that morning when I was making the chart to determine where the players would stand. Hearing myself read the list of names was unbelievable …*Bill Walton stands next to Wilt Chamberlain, Chamberlain next to Willis Reed…* I remember thinking, "Wow. This is truly amazing."

The biggest challenge in taking this photograph was time. We only had a little

more than five minutes to get everyone suited up in their NBA at 50 leather jackets and arranged to execute the shot. We had a total of 47 players present and every second counted. Shooting a large group portrait is always challenging in trying to keep everyone's attention. The best frame happened to be the most fitting. The only player talking and not looking at the camera was, appropriately enough, Charles Barkley, the group's class clown.

This was a once-in-a-lifetime portrait shoot for this lifelong fan of the game that will always be cherished.

—*Nathaniel S. Butler,*
NBA Senior Official Staff Photographer

I'M A BIG BELIEVER in karma. What goes around, comes around. So on my first trip to Chicago to shoot Michael Jordan and the Bulls, I wanted to make sure I was maintaining good karma. I arrived at the United Center early to set up my remote camera behind the glass as I always do. I was later told that my camera had to be moved to the other end of the court. So, I went with the flow, moving my camera and my courtside position. Fortunately that fateful switch put me in perfect position to capture this famous photograph.

During the second half of the game the Bulls were blowing out the Golden State Warriors by 20-plus. It wasn't a good game to shoot because of the point differential and the fact that Michael didn't see many minutes. All of a sudden, the ball spurts out of the key. I instinctively followed it as it headed out of bounds when suddenly Rodman comes flying after it. Making the picture was pure reflex. If I thought about it I would have missed it. I think this image captures the essence of Dennis: athleticism, drive,

unpredictability, and craziness. After all, who else would risk injury diving like this for a loose ball with his team up by 20?

—*Sam Forencich, NBA Photographer*

SHOOTING FOR GREATNESS
WITH OPENING TIP STILL HOURS AWAY, LARRY BIRD SHOWS
WHERE CHAMPIONS ARE MADE—ON THE PRACTICE COURT.
BIRD'S METICULOUS GAME-DAY PREPARATION HELPED ADD THREE
CHAMPIONSHIP BANNERS TO THE ALREADY SWELLING BOSTON
GARDEN RAFTERS DURING HIS 13 HALL-OF-FAME SEASONS.

OUT OF REACH

WILT CHAMBERLAIN NOT ONLY DEMONSTRATES
UNIQUE FORM BUT ALSO A GLIMPSE OF HIS
ENORMOUS WINGSPAN AS HE FLIPS THE BALL JUST
BARELY OVER THE OUTSTRETCHED RIGHT ARM OF
WILLIS REED OF THE NEW YORK KNICKS.

CENTER OF ATTENTION

THE LATEST IN THE LINE OF GREAT LAKERS'
BIG MEN ARRIVES IN 1996 AS SHAQUILLE O'NEAL
IS WELCOMED INTO THE EXCLUSIVE FRATERNITY
BY KAREEM ABDUL-JABBAR [FAR LEFT]
AND GEORGE MIKAN. THIS RARE GET-TOGETHER
IS THE FIRST AND ONLY TIME ALL THREE LEGENDARY
BIG MEN GATHERED FOR A PORTRAIT.

CATCH ME IF YOU CAN

A FOCUSED ALLEN IVERSON ATTEMPTS A LAYUP
FOR A QUICK SCORE ONLY TO BE FOLLOWED BY
A FIERCELY DETERMINED, HAND WAVING, VINCE
CARTER, WHO CLEARLY HAS OTHER PLANS.

WITH AUTHORITY

THE THROUGH-THE-GLASS PERSPECTIVE REVEALS
THE INTENSE LOOK OF DETERMINATION ON THE
FACE OF LATRELL SPREWELL AS HE ZOOMS IN
FOR AN AUTHORITATIVE DUNK.

RIVALRIES, PRESENT AND PAST

THE HOTLY CONTESTED BATTLE FOR POSITION AND LOOK OF ANTICIPATION SYMBOLIZES
THE BUDDING RIVALRY BETWEEN VINCE CARTER AND KOBE BRYANT (ABOVE) WHILE
LEGENDS LARRY BIRD AND MAGIC JOHNSON (RIGHT) ARE FOREVER LINKED AS ONE OF THE
GREATEST INDIVIDUAL RIVALRIES IN NBA HISTORY. BIRD AND MAGIC AND THEIR
RESPECTIVE TEAMS—CELTICS AND LAKERS—CLASHED 37 TIMES DURING THEIR CAREERS,
WITH L.A. OWNING A 22-15 ADVANTAGE IN GAMES AND 2-1 ADVANTAGE IN CHAMPIONSHIPS.

DESIRE
DENNIS RODMAN STEALS A PAGE OUT OF A
DAVID COPPERFIELD MAGIC ACT AS THIS BRILLIANT
PHOTO CAPTURES HIS DESIRE TO POSSESS THE
BALL WHILE SUSPENDED IN AIR. THE FANS IN THE
COURTSIDE SEATS, INCLUDING THE LATE MOVIE CRITIC
GENE SISKEL [CENTER], LOOK ON IN DISBELIEF.

FAMILIAR FOES

THE STATUESQUE POSES BY JOHN HAVLICEK AND
JERRY WEST, CAPTURED DURING A PAUSE IN THE
ACTION BETWEEN THE CELTICS AND LAKERS, APPEAR
TO REVEAL THE DEEP MUTUAL ADMIRATION AND
RESPECT THE TWO RIVALS HAD FOR ONE ANOTHER
THROUGHOUT THEIR STORIED CAREERS.

MIRROR IMAGE

AN ARTISTIC REFLECTION CAPTURING THE GAME'S
FLUID MOTION BEAMS OFF THE POLISHED COURT OF
THIS EARLY 1970S IMAGE FEATURING JERRY WEST
TRIGGERING A LAKERS FAST BREAK, WITH TEAMMATE
GAIL GOODRICH FILLING THE LANE.

THE CAPTAIN RETURNS

MADISON SQUARE GARDEN ERUPTS IN CHEERS
AS WILLIS REED MAKES HIS SPINE-TINGLING
GAME 7 ENTRANCE AT THE 1970 NBA FINALS
AGAINST THE LOS ANGELES LAKERS. REED MISSED
THE PREVIOUS GAME DUE TO A TORN MUSCLE
BUT RETURNED TO THE FINAL GAME OF THE
SERIES AND PROVIDED THE KNICKS WITH ENOUGH
INSPIRATION TO CLAIM THEIR FIRST CHAMPIONSHIP.

NO FEAR
THE DIMINUTIVE ALLEN IVERSON TAKES TO THE AIR
AND SHOWS HIS TREMENDOUS HEART AND COURAGE
IN VENTURING UNDER THE BASKET WHILE ELUDING
THE OUTSTRETCHED ARM OF TIM DUNCAN.

LOOK OUT BELOW!
COREY MAGGETTE DUCKS FOR COVER
AS JEFF FOSTER DISPLAYS ASTONISHING
ATHLETICISM AND BALLETIC GRACE IN HIS
ATTEMPT TO DUNK THE BALL.

IN YOUR FACE
FOLLOWING SPREAD:
THIS EYE-CATCHING PERSPECTIVE OFFERS AN
UP CLOSE AND PERSONAL VIEW OF KEVIN
GARNETT AS HE IS ABOUT TO UNLOAD A
"KG SPECIAL" DURING THE 1998 NBA ALL-STAR
GAME IN NEW YORK'S MADISON SQUARE GARDEN.

A LEGACY OF PASSION

THIS PHOTO OF THE LATE, GREAT DRAZEN PETROVIC OF THE NEW JERSEY NETS FOREVER MEMORIALIZES THE EMOTION, SPIRIT, AND PASSION IN WHICH HE PLAYED THE GAME HE DEARLY LOVED. PETROVIC'S ZEST FOR EXCELLENCE EARNED HIM THE REPUTATION AS ONE OF THE NBA'S GREATEST SHOOTERS AND HARDEST WORKERS.

HOME COURT

FROM HIS WORN LEATHER BASKETBALL SHOES, THE MILESTONE BASKETBALL, AND HIS FAVORITE CHAIR, THIS ELEGANT, UNDERSTATED TRIBUTE TO THE LATE PETE MARAVICH EVOKES THE HALL-OF-FAMER'S PRESENCE. PHOTOGRAPHED ON HIS HOME SOIL IN LOUISIANA, THIS PEACEFUL IMAGE OFFERS QUITE A CONTRAST TO THE FLASHY BASKETBALL PERSONA OF PISTOL PETE, ONE OF THE GREATEST CREATIVE TALENTS IN NBA HISTORY.

10,000 Points
FEB. 26, 1976

THE PHANTOM TEAMMATE

THE ATHLETICISM AND PASSING SKILLS OF 7'-0" BIG
MAN TIM DUNCAN ARE ON FULL DISPLAY IN HIS
ATTEMPT TO EVADE SHAQUILLE O'NEAL IN THE PAINT.

A DREAM FINISH

KNOWN AS ONE OF THE GAME'S STRONGEST
FINISHERS, THIS PHOTO CONVEYS THE
DETERMINATION OF HAKEEM OLAJUWON
ABOUT TO SCORE YET ANOTHER BASKET
AS SHAWN KEMP AND THE REST OF HIS
SEATTLE TEAMMATES WATCH IN AWE.

AN ALL-STAR WELCOME
PREVIOUS SPREAD:
MICHAEL JORDAN WARMLY GREETS ALLEN IVERSON
AS HE STEPS OFF THE COURT AT HALF-TIME DURING
THE 2001 NBA ALL-STAR GAME IN WASHINGTON, D.C.,
AS A BEAMING STEPHON MARBURY WAITS
HIS TURN TO BE GREETED BY THE NBA LEGEND.

FAN FAVORITES

EAGER FANS CLAMOR FOR SIGNATURES OF
THEIR FAVORITE NBA HEROES KEVIN GARNETT
(OPPOSITE PAGE) AND STEPHON MARBURY, WHO ARE
MORE THAN HAPPY TO OBLIGE THE SURGE OF
REQUESTS DURING PRE-GAME WARM-UPS.

FACES OF THE NBA

PORTRAITS REVEAL DIFFERENT ASPECTS OF PLAYERS'
PERSONALITIES, WHETHER IT'S A RAIN-SUITED GARY
PAYTON PROJECTING AN AURA OF BOLD CONFIDENCE,
THE SERIOUSNESS OF DAVID ROBINSON, THE PENSIVE
EXPRESSION OF TRACY McGRADY, OR THE SOUTH
BEACH CHIC OF ALONZO MOURNING.

HELLO, DOLLAR BILL

FRESH FROM HIS STUDIES AT OXFORD,
RHODES SCHOLAR AND PRINCETON GRAD
BILL BRADLEY ARRIVES IN NEW YORK IN 1967
FOR HIS ROOKIE SEASON WITH THE KNICKS.

RAREFIED AIR

JOHN STARKS INVADES MICHAEL JORDAN'S AIRSPACE
ON THIS SPECTACULAR, BASELINE DUNK AGAINST
HORACE GRANT AND MJ. THE MOVE ROCKED MADISON
SQUARE GARDEN AND PRESERVED NEW YORK'S 1993
PLAYOFF VICTORY AGAINST CHICAGO.

SCOTTIE BEAMS UP

IN THIS PIVOTAL PLAYOFF MOMENT BETWEEN
CHICAGO AND NEW YORK IN 1994 AT VENERABLE
CHICAGO STADIUM, SCOTTIE PIPPEN USES
QUICKNESS AND SHEER DETERMINATION IN
DELIVERING A DUNK—AND A STATEMENT—
TO PATRICK EWING AND THE KNICKS.

41

SPLISH-SPLASHING FUN
WHEN THEY WEREN'T REPRESENTING THE
U.S. MEN'S NATIONAL TEAM AT THE 1999
PRE-OLYMPIC QUALIFYING TOURNAMENT IN PUERTO
RICO, KEVIN GARNETT AND TIM HARDAWAY
MANAGED TO SHARE THEIR LOVE OF THE GAME
WITH YOUNG FANS IN A HOTEL POOL.

42

UP AND UNDER
IN A DISPLAY OF TRUE GRIT EN ROUTE TO A LAYUP,
STEPHON MARBURY INTERRUPTS THE SAN ANTONIO
BLOCK PARTY HOSTED BY PREMIER DEFENSIVE
PLAYERS DAVID ROBINSON [LEFT] AND TIM DUNCAN.

MAN IN MOTION
FOLLOWING SPREAD:
THE LIGHTNING-QUICK BALL-HANDLING SKILLS
OF TIM HARDAWAY ARE CAPTURED IN THIS
STROBOSCOPIC SEQUENTIAL VIEW OF
HIS FAMOUS CROSSOVER DRIBBLE.

A TRAPPED WARRIOR

DONYELL MARSHALL OF THE GOLDEN STATE
WARRIORS FINDS HIMSELF TRAPPED UNDER
THE 6'-11" BODY OF KEVIN GARNETT AS THE
MINNESOTA TIMBERWOLF FRANTICALLY
TRIES TO SECURE THE LOOSE BALL.

CLIPPER CROSSWINDS

GARY PAYTON OF THE SEATTLE SUPERSONICS
FINDS HIMSELF AFLOAT BETWEEN TWO CLIPPERS—
LAMAR ODOM [LEFT] AND MAURICE TAYLOR—
AS HE SETS SAIL TO THE BASKET.

MIGHTY MOUSE TAKES FLIGHT
DAMON STOUDAMIRE LIVES UP TO HIS NICKNAME
AND THE MIGHTY MOUSE TATTOO ON HIS
LEFT ARM AS HE LEAPS TO SAVE THE DAY
FOR THE PORTLAND TRAIL BLAZERS.

PICK POCKET
A DETERMINED JASON WILLIAMS LOCKS IN ON
JASON KIDD AS HE ATTEMPTS TO STRIP THE
BALL FROM THE ALL-STAR GUARD, WHO IS
UNDETERRED IN DRIVING TO THE BASKET.

A CHAMPIONSHIP STAND
PREVIOUS SPREAD:
THIS IMAGE OF A DETERMINED MICHAEL JORDAN
FROM THE 1991 NBA FINALS IS INDICATIVE OF
THE SERIES AS THE CHICAGO BULLS HOLD OFF
FIVE-TIME NBA CHAMPION MAGIC JOHNSON
AND THE LOS ANGELES LAKERS.

REBOUNDING KICK

TOM HEINSOHN WISELY MOVES OUT OF THE
WAY AS HIS TEAMMATE BILL RUSSELL SHOWS
AMAZING FLEXIBILITY IN A TAP-AND-KICK ROUTINE
VS. DETROIT IN THE INAUGURAL GAME AT THE NEW
MADISON SQUARE GARDEN ON FEBRUARY 14, 1968.

THE ULTIMATE RIVALS

WILT VS. RUSSELL IS CONSIDERED THE GREATEST
INDIVIDUAL RIVALRY IN NBA HISTORY. THE HALL
OF FAMERS MET 142 TIMES THROUGHOUT THEIR
CAREERS, WITH CHAMBERLAIN OWNING THE
STATISTICAL EDGE IN POINTS—28.7 TO
RUSSELL'S 14.5—AND REBOUNDS—28.7 TO 23.7.
BUT RUSSELL OWNED THE ULTIMATE ADVANTAGE
IN NBA CHAMPIONSHIPS—11 TO TWO.

CRUISING ALTITUDE
THE EXTRAORDINARY HANGTIME AND AERIAL
GRACE OF KOBE BRYANT SOARING TO THE HOOP
IS CAPTURED BRILLIANTLY BY THIS IMAGE FROM
HIGH ATOP THE GREAT WESTERN FORUM CEILING.

ROLE REVERSAL
GRANT HILL MIMICS THE SWAGGER AND CONFIDENCE OF THE CHAMP AS HE PLAYFULLY SPARS WITH MUHAMMAD ALI DURING ALI'S VISIT WITH THE TEAM USA MEN'S BASKETBALL PLAYERS DURING THE 1996 SUMMER OLYMPICS IN ATLANTA.

OPEN ARMS
IN A DISPLAY OF BROTHERLY LOVE, PHILADELPHIA'S ALLEN IVERSON GRACIOUSLY GREETS VIEWERS WITH ARMS WIDE OPEN AND A WARM SMILE.

SIR CHARLES

CAPABLE OF DISPLAYING AN ANGELIC SMILE
IN THE WHIRLPOOL OR RAGING INTENSITY
ON-COURT, OUTSPOKEN FORWARD CHARLES
BARKLEY WAS AS FAMOUS FOR HIS SHOOT-FROM-
THE-LIP COMMENTARY AS HE WAS FOR HIS
EXTRAORDINARY BASKETBALL SKILLS.

DOUBLE TAKE

THE NUMBER MAY BE DIFFERENT BUT THE RESULT IS THE SAME. MICHAEL JORDAN'S TRADEMARK NO. 23 JERSEY WAS STOLEN PRIOR TO TIP-OFF—BUT AS THE STROBE FLASH ABOVE THE BALL INDICATES, THIS NEW NO. 12 STILL LEAVES OPPONENTS EARTHBOUND.

PEEK-A-BOO

DEE BROWN OF THE BOSTON CELTICS WOWED THE CHARLOTTE COLISEUM CROWD IN 1991 AND SCORED MAJOR POINTS FOR CREATIVITY WHEN HE WRAPPED HIS RIGHT ARM AROUND HIS HEAD FOR A PEEK-A-BOO DUNK. BROWN WAS LATER CROWNED SLAM-DUNK CHAMPION.

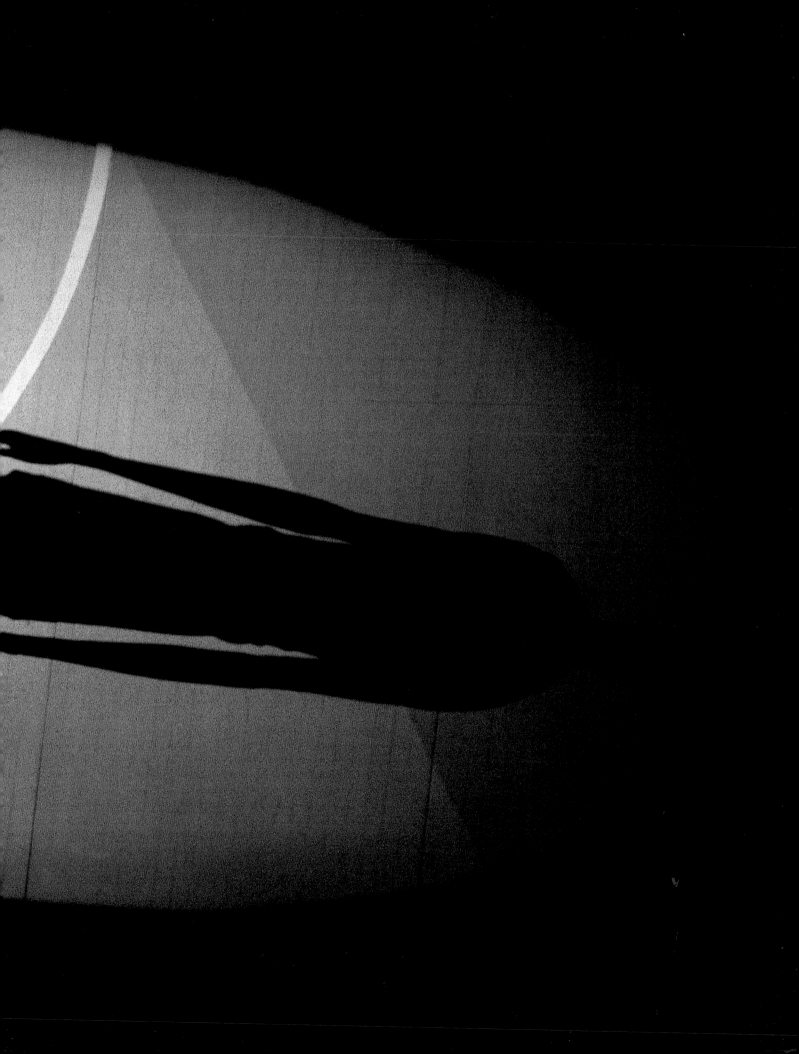

LOOMING PRESENCE
PREVIOUS SPREAD:
THE SPOTLIGHT CASTS AN IMMENSE SHADOW FROM
JULIUS ERVING, PARALLELING THE ENORMOUS
IMPACT HE HAD ON THE GAME. THE HALL OF FAMER'S
CREATIVE FLAIR AND INVENTIVE STYLE NOT ONLY
TRANSCENDED THE SPORT, BUT ALSO INFLUENCED
GENERATIONS OF FUTURE BASKETBALL PLAYERS.

ONLY THE BEGINNING
WHAT DO A BEST-SELLING AUTHOR ON MEMORY
TRAINING, A SUCCESSFUL BROADCASTER, A FRONT
OFFICE EXECUTIVE, A COACH AND A FORMER U.S.
SENATOR AND ONE-TIME PRESIDENTIAL CANDIDATE
HAVE IN COMMON? ALL WERE KEY CONTRIBUTORS
TO THE NEW YORK KNICKS 1973 NBA CHAMPIONSHIP
TEAM, WHICH SERVED AS A SPRINGBOARD FOR
FUTURE SUCCESS FOR JERRY LUCAS, WALT FRAZIER,
WILLIS REED, PHIL JACKSON, AND BILL BRADLEY.

BASKETBALL PRODIGIES

The preeminent members of the 1996 NBA Draft class have their game faces on in this feature shoot taken at the NBA's Rookie Orientation Program in the fall of 1996. Left to right: Marcus Camby, Ray Allen, Stephon Marbury, Kobe Bryant, Shareef Abdur-Rahim, Jermaine O'Neal, Kerry Kittles, Steve Nash, John Wallace, Antoine Walker, Samaki Walker.

FLIGHT CLEARANCE

TERENCE STANSBURY MADE A NAME FOR HIMSELF
AMONG NBA PLAYERS DURING HIS BRIEF THREE-YEAR
CAREER AS ONE OF THE MORE IMAGINATIVE AND
CREATIVE DUNKERS EVER TO PARTICIPATE IN THE
SLAM-DUNK CONTESTS. HIS INNOVATIVE DUNKS
EARNED HIM THREE STRAIGHT THIRD-PLACE FINISHES.

UNCONTESTED

THE PAINED LOOK ON RASHEED WALLACE'S FACE
SERVES AS AN INDICATOR OF WHAT IS ABOUT
TO UNFOLD—A CHRIS WEBBER TOMAHAWK SLAM
THAT WILL ROCK PORTLAND'S ROSE GARDEN.

OPPOSITES ATTRACT

At 7'-7", Manute Bol [left] clearly doesn't see eye to eye with his teammate, the 5'-3" Muggsy Bogues. The common bond between the tallest player in NBA history and one of the shortest, underscored by the triple-decker presentation of basketballs, is the game.

BEADS OF DETERMINATION

How can you measure the desire of an NBA player? Perhaps by the beads of perspiration that glisten and engulf the face of Shaquille O'Neal during his rookie season.

THE RINGMASTER
BILL RUSSELL'S SMILE IS AS DAZZLING AS
THE 11 NBA CHAMPIONSHIP RINGS—THE MOST
OF ANY NBA PLAYER THUS FAR—HE PROUDLY
DISPLAYS FOR THE CAMERA.

CHAMPIONSHIP ALLIANCE
BOSTON HEAD COACH RED AUERBACH AND
PERENNIAL ALL-STAR CENTER BILL RUSSELL HAD
PLENTY TO CELEBRATE AS THEY COLLABORATED
ON NINE CELTIC CHAMPIONSHIP TEAMS,
INCLUDING A STUNNING EIGHT IN A ROW.

LARRY'S LAST STAND

THE ANTICIPATION IS OVER FOR THE BOSTON GARDEN
FAITHFUL AS THEY GREET LARRY BIRD AS HE
APPROACHES THE FABLED PARQUET FLOOR FOR THE
LAST TIME PRIOR TO GAME 6 OF THE EASTERN
CONFERENCE SEMIFINALS BETWEEN THE CAVALIERS
AND THE CELTICS ON MAY 15, 1992.

A CHAMPIONSHIP EMBRACE
THE UNBRIDLED JOY AND SATISFACTION
EXPRESSED ON PAT RILEY'S FACE AS HE HUGS
MAGIC JOHNSON CAPTURES THE EUPHORIC MOOD
OF THE LAKERS LOCKER ROOM IN 1988 AS
THEY CELEBRATE BACK-TO-BACK TITLES.

ZO GOOD!
To the delight of his teammates and the
delirious Charlotte Coliseum crowd,
a fist-pumping Alonzo Mourning roars after
he buries the game-winner that eliminated
the Boston Celtics from the 1993 playoffs.

SHOW STOPPER

VINCE CARTER TOOK THE ART OF DUNKING
TO A HIGHER LEVEL DURING THE 2000
NBA.COM SLAM DUNK CONTEST WITH THIS
BETWEEN-THE-LEGS AERIAL MASTERPIECE THAT
PUSHED THE BOUNDARIES OF HANGTIME.

HOUSE CALL

HOW HIGH CAN JULIUS SKY? A LOW-ANGLE
PERSPECTIVE CAPTURES THE GRACE, STYLE, AND
SHOWMANSHIP THAT MADE ERVING—DR. J—ONE
OF THE PREEMINENT DUNKERS IN NBA HISTORY.

CROWNING ACHIEVEMENT

AN EMOTIONAL MICHAEL JORDAN CLUTCHES THE
LARRY O'BRIEN TROPHY AS HIS PROUD FATHER,
JAMES JORDAN, SHARES IN THE JOY OF HIS SON'S
FIRST NBA CHAMPIONSHIP IN 1991. MICHAEL'S
OUTPOURING OF EMOTION CAPPED A SEVEN-
SEASON-LONG CLIMB FOR THE TITLE.

VICTORY CIGAR

BASKING IN THE GLOW OF SOME OF THE
CHAMPIONSHIP BANNERS HE WAS RESPONSIBLE
FOR AS COACH AND GENERAL MANAGER OF
THE BOSTON CELTICS, RED AUERBACH ENJOYS
HIS TRADEMARK VICTORY CIGAR.

HIGHSTEPPING

WHO SAYS 6'-9" POWER FORWARDS AREN'T LIMBER?
KARL MALONE OF THE UTAH JAZZ REFUTES SUCH
A NOTION AS HE HAULS IN A REBOUND ON ONE LEG
WHILE HIGH-STEPPING WITH THE OTHER.

HANG GLIDING

ALL THE PLAYERS CAN DO IS WATCH IN AWE AS THE
TORONTO RAPTORS' VINCE CARTER GLIDES THROUGH
THE AIR, FURTHER ILLUSTRATING HIS BREATHTAKING
ATHLETIC AND CREATIVE ABILITIES.

CHAMPIONSHIP REACTIONS

LAKERS KOBE BRYANT AND SHAQUILLE O'NEAL
ENTHUSIASTICALLY CELEBRATE THEIR FIRST
NBA CHAMPIONSHIP, PRESENTING QUITE A
CONTRAST TO THE CASUAL APPROACH TAKEN
BY VETERAN RON HARPER, WHO PREVIOUSLY
EARNED THREE RINGS IN CHICAGO, AS HE
CALMLY WALKS AWAY WITH THE GAME BALL.

HEAD GAMES

THE PLAYFUL NATURE OF KEVIN GARNETT
CATCHING HIS ALL-STAR TEAMMATE TIM DUNCAN
OFF GUARD NOT ONLY REVEALS THE FUN-LOVING
SIDE OF THE MINNESOTA FORWARD'S PERSONALITY,
BUT ALSO CAPTURES THE CAMARADERIE THAT
EXISTS AMONG OPPOSING PLAYERS WHO
BECOME TEAMMATES ONE DAY EACH YEAR.

SHARP-DRESSED MAN

THE EASY-GOING, LAID-BACK PERSONALITY
OF ALLAN HOUSTON IS REFLECTED IN THIS
NEW YORK CITY PORTRAIT.

A BULLISH CURTAIN CALL

THE ANXIOUS FACES OF JAZZ FANS TELL THE
STORY IN THE FINAL MOMENTS OF GAME 6 OF
THE 1998 NBA FINALS. THEY AWAIT THE VERDICT
OF MICHAEL JORDAN'S JUMPER—A SHOT THAT
EVENTUALLY PUNCTURED UTAH'S CHAMPIONSHIP
HOPES AND PUNCTUATED MJ'S BRILLIANT
CAREER AS A CHICAGO BULL.

BASKETBALL BRILLIANCE

SEVERAL DIFFERENT ERAS CONVERGED TO CREATE A MOMENT OF CONTINUITY WITHIN THE BASKETBALL UNIVERSE DURING THE 1997 NBA ALL-STAR WEEKEND IN CLEVELAND. THE SCENE WAS CENTER COURT AT GUND ARENA AS THE GREATEST COLLECTION OF BASKETBALL TALENT IN THE HISTORY OF THE NBA MINGLED AND SWAPPED STORIES DURING THE LEAGUE'S 50TH ANNIVERSARY CELEBRATION. WHETHER IT WAS MICHAEL JORDAN MEETING WILT CHAMBERLAIN FOR THE FIRST TIME OR, SCOTTIE PIPPEN ASSISTING GEORGE MIKAN TO THE DAIS PRIOR TO THE PHOTO SESSION, THIS ONCE-IN-A-LIFETIME GATHERING OF THE 50 GREATEST PLAYERS IN NBA HISTORY WAS TRULY A TIMELESS MOMENT.
(SEE PAGE 4 FOR A LIST OF PLAYERS IN THE PICTURE.)

BRILLIANT DISGUISE

IT'S UNTHINKABLE! MAGIC JOHNSON DONNING THE COLORS OF THE ARCHENEMY? THE LAKER LEGEND MAKES A RARE EXCEPTION IN PAYING SPECIAL TRIBUTE TO HIS FRIEND AND RIVAL LARRY BIRD ON THE NIGHT THE CELTICS HONORED THE BOSTON LEGEND.

LOVE IT LIVE
WHETHER SITTING COURTSIDE OR IN THE LAST ROW,
FANS LOVE THE "LIVE EXPERIENCE" OF NBA
PLAYOFF BASKETBALL. HERE, SAN ANTONIO FANS
SHARE THE PASSION FROM THE FAR REACHES
OF THE ALAMODOME DURING THE KNICKS-SPURS
MATCH-UP IN THE 1999 NBA FINALS.

NOW YOU SEE IT...
JASON WILLIAMS OF THE SACRAMENTO KINGS
DEMONSTRATES HIS PASSING WIZARDRY WITH AN
OVER-THE-SHOULDER TOSS THAT TEMPORARILY
FREEZES HIS OPPONENTS.

HEAVEN SENT
THE CLOUDS GRACIOUSLY OPEN TO
WELCOME A ROOKIE BY THE NAME OF
STEPHON MARBURY AS HE GRACEFULLY BEGINS
HIS ASCENT TO NBA STARDOM IN 1996.

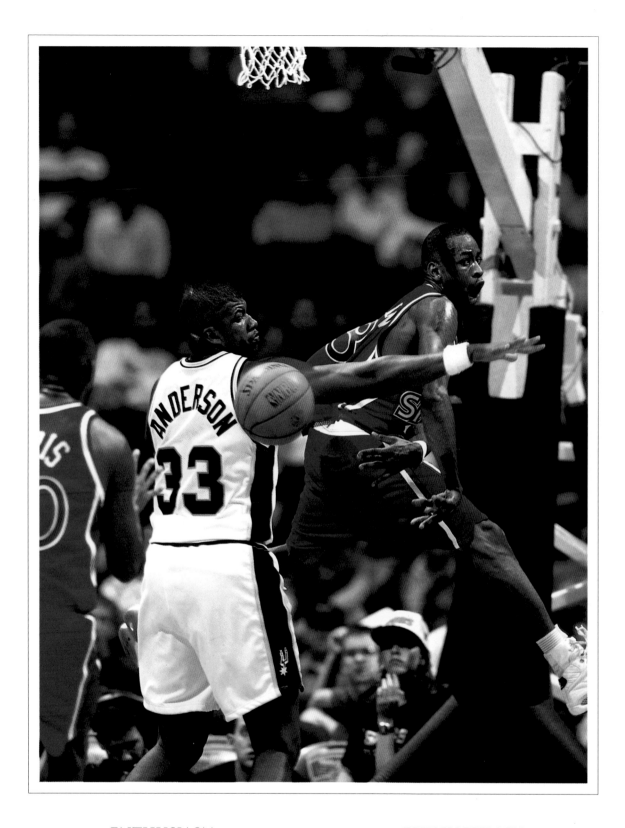

ENTHUSIASM

THE EXUBERANT PERSONALITY OF MAGIC JOHNSON LEAPS OFF THE PAGE IN THIS WALTER IOOSS, JR. PORTRAIT OF THE NBA LEGEND. MAGIC'S ENTHUSIASM, LOVE OF AND PASSION FOR THE GAME DEFINED HIM AS ONE OF THE GREAT NBA PERSONALITIES OF ALL TIME.

PHILLY PHLASH

FLYING ACROSS THE BASELINE, ALLEN IVERSON CATCHES THE SPURS' CADILLAC ANDERSON FLAT-FOOTED WHILE WHIPPING A LASER NO-LOOK PASS TO HIS SIXER TEAMMATE.

CHANGING THE GAME
AT 6'-9" AND POSSESSING AN UNCANNY ALL-AROUND GAME, MAGIC JOHNSON REVOLUTIONIZED THE POINT GUARD POSITION WITH HIS ABILITY TO DISSECT DEFENSES IN DRIVING TO THE HOOP.

INCOMING
KEVIN GARNETT ZEROES IN FOR AN EXCLAMATION DUNK AS THE REMAINING NINE PLAYERS ON THE COURT EAGERLY AWAIT THE DELIVERY.

THE GRIM REAPER

GIVING NEW MEANING TO HOME-COURT ADVANTAGE, THIS MENACING HALLOWEEN DECORATION SEEMS TO ENERGIZE ANTAWN JAMISON AND THE GOLDEN STATE WARRIORS ON OPENING NIGHT, OCTOBER 31, 2000.

ROYAL TREATMENT

AN OUTPOURING OF CONFETTI AND EMOTION ERUPTS FROM ARCO ARENA FANS AS CHRIS WEBBER WALKS VICTORIOUSLY TO THE LOCKER ROOM AFTER THE KINGS VICTORY OVER THE LOS ANGELES LAKERS. THE VICTORY SENT THE FIRST-ROUND SERIES OF THE 2000 NBA PLAYOFFS TO A FIFTH AND DECIDING GAME IN L.A.

FRIENDLY FOES

THE LIGHTHEARTED EXCHANGE BETWEEN
EASTERN CONFERENCE ALL-STARS VINCE
CARTER AND ALLAN HOUSTON AND WESTERN
CONFERENCE FOE KEVIN GARNETT AT THE 2000
NBA ALL-STAR GAME IN OAKLAND REFLECTS
THE CLOSENESS AMONG PLAYERS.

ATTITUDE

PALMING A BASKETBALL WITH EACH HAND,
ROOKIE LAMAR ODOM DISPLAYS AN AURA OF
CONFIDENCE AS HE SETS OUT TO MAKE HIS MARK IN
THE NBA. THIS PORTRAIT OF THE LOS ANGELES
CLIPPERS' 1999 FIRST-ROUND PICK WAS TAKEN
AT THE LEAGUE'S ROOKIE TRANSITION PROGRAM.

BASELINE HUSTLE
ELGIN BAYLOR, ONE OF THE NBA'S
ORIGINAL HIGH FLYERS, REMAINS
EARTHBOUND ON THIS MOVE AS HE BEATS
HIS KNICK DEFENDER TO THE BASKET.

UNTANGLED WEBB
CHRIS WEBBER OF THE GOLDEN STATE WARRIORS
WEAVES AN UNCONTESTED PATH TO THE BASKET
DURING HIS ROOKIE SEASON IN PREPARATION
FOR AN EMPHATIC POWER SLAM.

GROUNDED
THE SERIOUS LOOK EXPRESSED ON
DAMON STOUDAMIRE'S GAME FACE REFLECTS
OFF THE GLISTENING COURT AS HE MENTALLY
AND PHYSICALLY PREPARES FOR A GAME.

WE DID IT!
THE THRILL OF ACCOMPLISHMENT IS CLEARLY
EXPRESSED BY HOUSTON BACKCOURTMATES
CUTTINO MOBLEY AND STEVE FRANCIS, WHO DISPLAY
YOUTHFUL EXUBERANCE AT A ROCKETS HOME GAME.

SPECIAL DELIVERY
KARL MALONE—THE MAILMAN—RECEIVES PLENTY
OF STYLE POINTS ON THIS DUNK ATTEMPT AS HE
STRIKES A POSE FOR THE PHOTOGRAPHER.

GENTLE GIANTS

THE JOYFUL EXPRESSIONS OF SHAQUILLE O'NEAL
AND HAKEEM OLAJUWON REFLECT THE MUTUAL
RESPECT AND ADMIRATION THE TWO RIVALS AND
FRIENDS HAVE FOR ONE ANOTHER. THIS PRESCIENT
PHOTO FORESHADOWED THE 1995 NBA FINALS,
WHICH PITTED O'NEAL'S ORLANDO MAGIC AGAINST
OLAJUWON'S HOUSTON ROCKETS.

ICE, ICE, BABY

THE SMILE ON GEORGE GERVIN'S FACE SHOWS
DELIGHT IN THE ICE-SCULPTURED BASKETBALLS
PREPARED BY NBA PHOTOGRAPHERS FOR THE
SPECIAL NBA AT 50 PORTRAIT SHOOT IN 1996.
GERVIN EARNED THE NICKNAME "ICEMAN" FOR
HIS SMOOTH AND GRACEFUL SCORING ABILITY.

CENTER STAGE
FOLLOWING SPREAD:
A COLORFUL LIGHTING SCHEME ILLUMINATES
THE PERFECT FREE THROW-SHOOTING FORM
AND ROBUST MUSCLE DEFINITION OF CHRIS MULLIN,
ONE OF THE NBA'S MOST ACCURATE SHOOTERS
FROM THE CHARITY STRIPE.

BASKETBALL ROYALTY

THE 1992 DREAM TEAM IS UNIVERSALLY CONSIDERED
THE GREATEST COLLECTION OF BASKETBALL TALENT
EVER ASSEMBLED. WITH A 43.8 AVERAGE MARGIN OF
VICTORY AND AN 8-0 RECORD EN ROUTE TO A
GOLD MEDAL, IT'S EASY TO UNDERSTAND WHY.

REIGN DANCE

SHAWN KEMP SHOWS IN THE 1996 NBA
ALL-STAR GAME THE FORM THAT EARNED HIM A
REPUTATION EARLIER IN HIS CAREER AS ONE OF
THE LEAGUE'S PREMIER FREQUENT FLYERS.

PREPARATION AND PAYOFF

BENEATH PAT RILEY'S SLICK, STYLISH APPEARANCE
IS A BLUE-COLLAR COACH WHO IS METICULOUS
IN PREPARATION. PREFERRING THE SOLITUDE OF
THE VISITORS LOCKER ROOM, RILEY AVOIDS
POTENTIAL DISTRACTIONS DURING HIS PRE-GAME
PREPARATION. HIS DISCIPLINED APPROACH HAS
PRODUCED FOUR NBA CHAMPIONSHIPS AND MORE
THAN 1,000 REGULAR-SEASON VICTORIES.

SCOREBOARD

LOOMING OVER JERRY SLOAN'S SHOULDER
IS THE UNITED CENTER SCOREBOARD,
THE SOURCE OF HIS DOUR EXPRESSION AS
THE UTAH JAZZ SUFFER THE WORSE LOSS
IN NBA FINALS HISTORY.

HANGING AROUND
PENNY HARDAWAY ADDS A CORKSCREW TOUCH
IN COMPLETING A MAGICAL REVERSE DUNK,
MUCH TO THE DELIGHT OF THE ORLANDO FANS.

A PHILLY WRAPAROUND
ALLEN IVERSON DEMONSTRATES HIS UNDERRATED
PASSING SKILLS WITH THIS BEHIND-THE-BACK
LASER THAT CATCHES EVERYONE OFF GUARD
EXCEPT HIS AWAITING TEAMMATE.

THE BIG SNORKELER

EVEN IN THE SOOTHING HAWAIIAN WATERS,
SHAQUILLE O'NEAL'S PRESENCE LOOMS LARGE
AS HE CATCHES HIS BREATH AFTER SWIMMING
WITH THE OTHER BIG FISH.

SETTING SAIL

THE LAKERS QUEST FOR ANOTHER TITLE BEGAN
WITH THIS TEAM PHOTO SHOOT AT NEWPORT BEACH
PRIOR TO THE START OF THE 1987-88 SEASON.
THE LAKERS OVERCAME THE STORMY SEAS OF
THE NBA PLAYOFFS TO BECOME THE FIRST TEAM
IN 19 YEARS TO REPEAT AS NBA CHAMPIONS.

KING OF NEW YORK
PLAYFULLY DONNING A ROYAL WARDROBE
OUTSIDE LEGENDARY MADISON SQUARE GARDEN,
PROLIFIC SCORER BERNARD KING CLAIMS NEW
YORK'S BASKETBALL THRONE IN THE MID-'80S.

STRICTLY BUSINESS
LATRELL SPREWELL OF THE NEW YORK KNICKS
APPEARS TO EMERGE FROM THE DARKNESS IN A
BRILLIANTLY LIT PHOTOGRAPH CAPTURING THE
GUARD'S NO-NONSENSE APPROACH TO THE GAME.

COURT VISION

PEERING THROUGH A LAYER OF DEFENDERS,
JASON KIDD'S EYES EMPHASIZE THE IMPORTANCE
OF COURT VISION AS HE STUDIES THE OPPOSITION,
CALCULATING A WAY TO DELIVER ONE OF HIS
CUSTOMARY PINPOINT PASSES TO A TEAMMATE.

SUDDEN IMPACT

POSSESSING PRECISE BODY CONTROL,
JOHN STOCKTON USES HIS ATHLETICISM TO
STOP IN MIDAIR AND DELIVER THE BALL TO
LONGTIME TEAMMATE KARL MALONE BEFORE
COLLIDING WITH DETLEF SCHREMPF.

PUT IT THERE

CENTERS NATE THURMOND AND DAVE COWENS
DEMONSTRATE THE FINER POINTS OF SPORTSMANSHIP
PRIOR TO ENGAGING IN AN ON-COURT BATTLE.
THE WARM EXCHANGE REVEALS THE DEEP RESPECT
BOTH PLAYERS HAVE FOR ONE ANOTHER AND THE
BROTHERHOOD THAT EXISTS AMONG NBA PLAYERS.

T-MAC-NIFICENT!

TRACY MCGRADY STOLE THE SHOW AT THE 2002 NBA ALL-STAR GAME WHEN HE THREW A PASS TO HIMSELF THAT RICOCHETED OFF THE BACKBOARD. MCGRADY THEN FLEW BY THREE DEFENDERS FOR A SPECTACULAR SLAM DUNK THAT HAD THE CROWD BUZZING LONG AFTER THE PLAY WAS OVER.

CHOCOLATE THUNDER ERUPTS

DARRYL DAWKINS, THE OUTRAGEOUS, FLAMBOYANT AND COMEDIC CENTER, OWNED A MULTITUDE OF NICKNAMES AS A PLAYER AND ALWAYS USED HIS SHEER FORCE IN DELIVERING SLAM DUNKS. OFTENTIMES, HIS DUNKS VISIBLY RATTLED BOTH BASKETS AND HIS OPPONENTS, EARNING HIM THE NICKNAME CHOCOLATE THUNDER.

ROARING WITH APPROVAL

ALL-STAR CENTER PATRICK EWING'S TRADEMARK
SCOWL AND LOOK OF PIERCING INTENSITY GIVE WAY
TO THE EMOTIONAL RELEASE OF THE MOMENT.

ZO STRONG

NOT EVEN TWO DETROIT PISTON DEFENDERS COULD
DETER ALL-STAR CENTER ALONZO MOURNING FROM
MUSCLING IN AND COMPLETING A POWERFUL DUNK.

ORLANDO'S PIANO MAN

WHEN HE'S NOT PLAYING BASKETBALL,
GRANT HILL ENJOYS TICKLING THE IVORIES
AT HOME. THE ORLANDO MAGIC FORWARD
DOESN'T NEED TO LOOK FAR FOR INSPIRATION:
HE'S MARRIED TO GRAMMY NOMINATED
R&B SINGER TAMIA.

GRATEFUL RED

BESIDES BASKETBALL, BILL WALTON'S GREAT
PASSION IS THE MUSIC OF THE GRATEFUL DEAD.
THE HALL-OF-FAMER AND TWO-TIME NBA CHAMPION
DREW INSPIRATION FROM THE LEGENDARY
BAND AND MADE THEIR MUSIC A MAJOR PART
OF HIS GAME-DAY ROUTINE.

BLOCK PARTY

SHAWN MARION DISPLAYS PERFECT FORM
IN SHOWING OFF HIS AMAZING VERTICAL
LEAP AS HE FORCEFULLY REJECTS
ELTON BRAND'S DUNK ATTEMPT.

FAN APPRECIATION

THE SMILE ON THE FACE OF THIS YOUNG FAN
SAYS IT ALL AS PHILADELPHIA SUPERSTAR ALLEN
IVERSON MAKES A PERSONAL CONNECTION.

ELATION AND REFLECTION

SHAQUILLE O'NEAL BELLOWS AMID A CHAMPAGNE
SHOWER IN CELEBRATING THE LAKERS BACK-TO-BACK
TITLES (LEFT) WHILE HIS TEAMMATE KOBE BRYANT (ABOVE)
CHOOSES A MORE SERENE APPROACH IN COMMEMORATING
THE MAGNITUDE OF HIS TEAM'S HISTORIC ACCOMPLISHMENT.

MEMORIAL DAY MIRACLE

PANDEMONIUM ENSUES AFTER SEAN ELLIOTT
NAILS A GAME-WINNING THREE-POINTER WITH
9.9 SECONDS LEFT IN GAME 2 OF THE 1999
WESTERN CONFERENCE FINALS AGAINST THE
PORTLAND TRAIL BLAZERS. ELLIOTT'S HEROICS
HELPED THE SPURS TO A SWEEP OF PORTLAND.

ICY STARE

WITH THE COOL BRAVADO OF A SHOOTER
REMINISCENT OF AN OLD WEST GUNFIGHTER,
GEORGE "ICEMAN" GERVIN WAS ONE OF THE
MOST PROLIFIC SCORERS IN NBA HISTORY.

SIGNATURE GOGGLES

THEY ARE AS RECOGNIZABLE AS HIS FAMED SKY-HOOK
AND HAVE BEEN A FIXTURE IN HALL-OF-FAMER KAREEM
ABDUL-JABBAR'S STORIED CAREER. APPROPRIATELY,
THE LAST PAIR OF GOGGLES WORN BY THE NBA
LEGEND ARE ON DISPLAY AT THE BASKETBALL HALL
OF FAME IN SPRINGFIELD, MASSACHUSETTS.

ANGUISH

PERHAPS NO OTHER PLAYER WAS CONSUMED BY
THE DESIRE TO WIN MORE THAN HALL-OF-FAMER
JERRY WEST. LEGENDARY LAKER BROADCASTER
CHICK HEARN ONCE SAID THAT HE HAS NEVER
SEEN A PLAYER TAKE A LOSS HARDER THAN WEST.
IN WEST'S 13 NBA SEASONS, THE LAKERS REACHED
THE NBA FINALS NINE TIMES—AND LOST EIGHT OF
THOSE SERIES, MUCH TO HIS DISMAY.

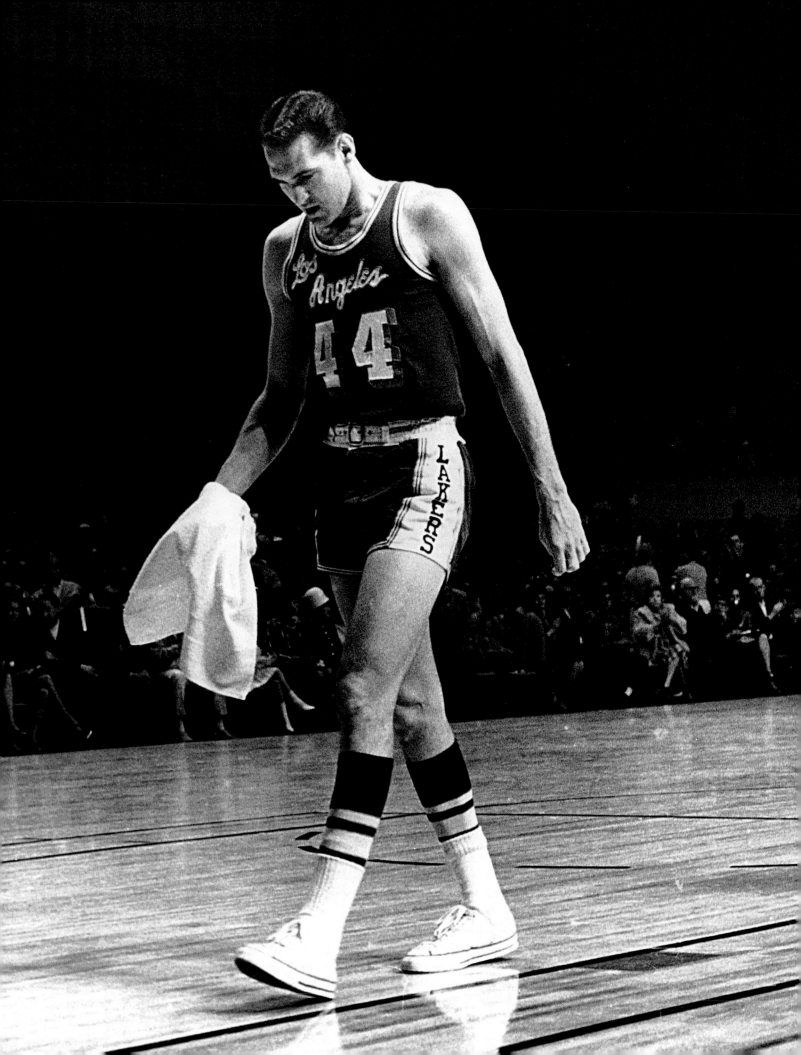

FAN APPRECIATION
THE EXPRESSION ON THE YOUNG FAN'S
FACE PROVES THAT RAY ALLEN CAN SCORE
PLENTY OF POINTS OFF THE COURT AS WELL.
THE NBA ALL-STAR GUARD MADE THIS
PERSONAL CONNECTION AT THE MILWAUKEE
BUCKS HOME, THE BRADLEY CENTER.

GARDEN PARTY
THE NEW YORK LOVE FEST BEGINS AS
PATRICK EWING TRIUMPHANTLY EXTENDS HIS
ARMS TO THE THUNDEROUS MADISON SQUARE
GARDEN OVATION AFTER NEW YORK'S GAME 7
TRIUMPH AGAINST THE INDIANA PACERS IN
THE 1994 EASTERN CONFERENCE FINALS.

MENTAL PREPARATION
PREVIOUS SPREAD:
The Boston Garden lights combined with the glow of the shot clock emit a supernatural aura as Celtic great John Havlicek mentally prepares to enter the game.

SPREAD EAGLE
The extraordinary levitation and body language clearly evokes the athleticism of Corey Maggette, who also shows great basketball awareness with a midair look down court for an open teammate.

BICYCLE KICK

THE ASTONISHING BODY LANGUAGE AND AGILITY
OF DENNIS RODMAN IS CAPTURED PERFECTLY IN
THIS MIDAIR SHOT, WHICH DOESN'T LEAVE ANY DOUBT
AS TO WHO OWNS POSSESSION OF THE BALL.

BUDDY SYSTEM
Teammates on the court, friends off, Kobe Bryant and Shaquille O'Neal share a humorous moment in this behind-the-scenes look at the two Lakers.

CHAMPIONSHIP LOOK
NBA Championships are won on the practice court—as Scottie Pippen's body language and facial expression indicate clearly.

PERSONAL REFLECTIONS

WHETHER IT'S THE BOASTFUL ATHLETIC DISPLAY
OF JERMAINE O'NEAL, THE PLAYFULNESS OF BARON
DAVIS, THE POISED LOOK OF JASON KIDD, OR
THE WARMTH OF JERRY STACKHOUSE'S SMILE,
A VARIETY OF EXPRESSIONS REFLECT THE DIVERSE
PERSONALITIES OF NBA PLAYERS.

L.A. STYLE

THE PICTURESQUE SETTING OF DOWNTOWN
LOS ANGELES AND THE BEAUTIFUL BLUE SKY
PERSONIFY A COOL SOUTHERN CALIFORNIA STYLE
THAT CLEARLY SUITS THE ULTRACOOL KOBE BRYANT.

WUNDERDUNK

THE ATHLETICISM AND FLUID MOVES OF 7'-0"
FORWARD DIRK NOWITZKI ARE ON FULL DISPLAY
AS THE DALLAS ALL-STAR SHOWS ONE FACET
OF HIS ALL-AROUND GAME.

HORNET'S NEST

DINO RADJA FINDS HIMSELF SURROUNDED
BY A BUZZ OF ACTIVITY AS MULTIPLE
HORNETS SURROUND HIM IN THE HONEYCOMB
LANE AT THE HIVE.

BULLISH CELEBRATION

A MARDI GRAS-STYLE PARTY ERUPTS IN CHICAGO
AS ROOKIE TYSON CHANDLER ENTHUSIASTICALLY
CELEBRATES A REGULAR-SEASON VICTORY ON
THE BACK OF FELLOW ROOKIE TRENTON HASSELL.
THE UNBRIDLED JOY EXHIBITED BY THE PLAYERS
REFLECTS THEIR PASSION FOR WINNING.

THE MATRIX

DEMONSTRATING HOW HE GOT HIS CINEMATIC
NICKNAME, PHOENIX SUNS FORWARD SHAWN
"THE MATRIX" MARION OVERPOWERS HIS
OPPONENT, SHOWCASING HIS TREMENDOUS
DRIVE IN BURSTING TO THE BASKET.

LARRY...THANK YOU
13 GREAT SEASO

A NIGHT TO REMEMBER
PREVIOUS SPREAD:
LARRY BIRD TAKES A MOMENT TO REFLECT DURING
THE FEBRUARY 4, 1993 RETIREMENT CEREMONY
HONORING THE HALL-OF-FAMER. BIRD IS ONE
OF THE MOST BELOVED CELTICS IN THAT
FRANCHISE'S STORIED HISTORY.

CURTAIN CALL
THE COMPETITIVE DRIVE AND PASSION FOR
THE GAME LURED MICHAEL JORDAN AND
HIS MASTERFUL MOVES BACK TO THE NBA,
THIS TIME AS A WASHINGTON WIZARD.